ONE FOR SORROW, T

Caleb Nichols is a poet and musician from a working class family in California. His poetry and prose has been published in places like the *New England Review, 14 Poems, Poetry Wales, Redivider,* and *45th Parallel.* Caleb's rock opera *Ramon* was released on indie record label Kill Rock Stars in 2022 and he's toured North American and Europe in support of it and other KRS releases. A best of the net nominee, and a recipient of an Academy of American Poets University prize, Caleb is a PhD candidate in Creative Writing at Bangor University in North Wales.

CONTENTS

ISBN: 978-1-916938-27-4

The author has asserted their right to be identified as the author of this Work in accordance with the Copyright, Designs and Patents Act 1988

Cover designed by Aaron Kent

Edited and Typeset by Aaron Kent

Broken Sleep Books Ltd
PO BOX 102
Llandysul
SA44 9BG

One for Sorrow, Two for Joy

Caleb Nichols

Broken Sleep Books

SING

maybe I'm just here
to listen to the wind

for solitude
and what silence can be

salvaged from the noise
I'm reaching

out with all my senses
ear to the howling

night gathering
eyes and fresh salt scents

I'm seeing more clearly
each drop

of day tasting
each dram of this time

I'm touching
one hand to the other

flexing my lonely
my longing my hope

when I sing
I sing for me

& once the candle's lit
I keep it burning

KING'S CROSS TRAVELODGE ROYAL SCOT

Rain-blurred
London
a windowpane
a wet cough
from a passing cab
& pigeons jaywalking

Piccadilly

clean speckled
gem blue sky

2 days in
Marchmont

nothing better
than to

circumambulate

to leaf
past shop windows
like pages
yes the hush
& psither psither
of October city streets

MENAI STRAIT

All answers are answers to all questions."
— John Cage

cliff whisperings sink
into sea shush
& bric a brac crunch
shells mainly
slate shards
three pysgod
wibbli wobbli
clear plastic bottle
bright green sea glas
past the bath house
towards Garth Pier's
conch shaped huts
one fat swan necks
into the water
guzzles something

I keep asking myself
where I fit into this
landscape

a lime green acorn
lodged in sea-slimed rock
a pop of flaming autumn
limbs erupting from the bank
streaked across the grey
sky water reflection

I'm just this
pair of green trainers
yellow flannel shirt
& faded black denim
trundling

just this question
asked to nothing
not silence not self
no such thing

BUS STOP, GWYNEDD

two boys kissing
in the shelter of a bus stop
in the shadow of a cemetery
along the A5 towards Penrhyn
and the Afon Cegin
                 Kitchen River
one lad clutches the other's
jaw cupped in both hands
his hips flexed forward
the other's leant back
as if to say

how far will you go?
how far will you follow?

RESPAIR

so most days
       I follow my feet
           through thickets
               into holloways
           over gentle hills
        always beneath this
  soft morning light
         the paths
           switchback I follow
           I hope
         they don't veer too far upwards
       I've a fear of heights although
I've always thought *fear of* or *phobia*
           to be such a misnomer
                   one Welsh word for fear is *ofn*
              which derives from a celtic word for *shiver*
                   and yes that's right
                      this thing
                     it's located
                      deep
                    in the body
                  see
           I love a good view
        it's just that sometimes
      at a certain height part of me panics
    & then I get all wibbli wobbli
  & then my brain screams
let me out let me out let me out

13

or sometimes

take me home!

and then my heart kicks in

ADRENALIN

mad rush!

and I'm *off!*

It's not that I'm afraid

(my name means bravery)

it's just my body

being a body & miracle

of miracles I recover

I move on

TROS Y MÔR Y MAE FY NGHALON

I'm quite taken
with this land
of whimsical garden sheds
I can't seem to get enough
coffee or a strong enough
coffee I think I've become
a tea-drinker more quickly
than I had thought I would
and yes a slight trace of these
accents has crept
into my speech words like
sorted and questions phrased
in the affirmative
you alright
you OK
yeah
I'm good enough
with these pale-white
petals on these wet-black boughs
framing the paths
I find each day
paths punctured
by afternoon sun
a cigarette
more tea
oat milk

scone is pronounced scone
more often than *scawn*
& I can sort of begin
to make out the thickness
of Scouse of Scots but not
yet Welsh though I like
their bread & butter best
the best things I've seen
& heard & felt
are less lovely
with you away
& over the sea

LET THE POETS LIE

Some things live on in memory
and I want my memories preserved.
        I mean passed down, mouth to ear, to mouth.
        Yes, I've heard of telephone & that's partially the point
just because something has passed
doesn't mean it's not still subject
        to transformation. Take desire, because this is a poem:
        it passes, transforms into what it will— soul love
disdain, boredom, sorrow. The flame
flickers in whispers, tongue to lobe
        tells what it likes, what lies it loves, what it constructs.
        You & I, the old story: we weave it into what we need.

GLASLANC

A miracle

    of pleasure   *these are the days of*

that sort of thing

       wonder

    hands   thickness   thatch

& soft prickle   hands   span the circumference

      hands   tongue

bulk pressing into you   me   lightning strobing   over Anglesey

    rupturing   grey night   queer there was no thunder

      here in   margin-alia   *go on then*

      he grinned   *go on*

PLAYLIST

there's a spot on my neck
where I like to be kissed

a much much much younger
man kisses me on the spot

on my neck that I like & Peaches
sings *dick in the air let me see you*

put your put your dick in the air
& I'm laughmoaning his finger

pressing with just the right
pressure in just the right place

& Dry Cleaning chants *gym shorts*
show more & more & more

& I burst with laughter
with joy with infinity

VALENTINE

he said
you're the best looking man in this country

he said
I love your thighs

somehow knew exactly what to do with me
had skin like if marble could squish

I said
you have skin like   something   oh fuck I should be able

but I couldn't even come
close my language couldn't

approach the warm shore
I'd landed on

the surprising tincture
of sunlight spilling into morning

STATE OF EMERGENCY

after Frank O'Hara

He was coming over later to see me, say me, sort me
oh but the waves, those moorings now I'm lonely
useless I've spent the day in poems
& songs, indoors, out of sorts subsisting on memory's emotional
inscape   I & You   subsisting   sure but
denied   experience   say an outscape
an object   was Frank a fuckboy in his slick vessel
neither here nor there but hard alee his rudder   filled my
empty   for a little while sea met shore met mountain

SLATE AGE

I'm sat in this tree-
height window
watching

ravens
pica pica
rooks and gulls

in their daily arcs
leaves falling
to wet pavement

each day revealing
a bit more of
Anglesey

Beaumaris
Ynys Seiriol
the Irish Sea

each day unveiling
a bit more
landscape and barren

sky like the slate
just beneath
the green scruff

these hills wear
the same slate
grey as the sweats

the lad walking
up my garden path
is wearing

same slate
he wears after
stone-faced ghost

ONE FOR SORROW

the luxury

all morning

of watching

leaves ellipse

lift

twirl

pirouette

from the roof

to the sycamores

and a small sun-

back towards its branch

ravens swoop

past my window

back again

lifts off the ground

flutters

across the lane

coloured leaf

settles again

all day the pleasure

amber

of tracking

of a lone magpie   (one for sorrow)

tobacco   mustard   gathering

north wind   pushes clouds around   rust

                              leaf light

then   deep blue

plays sunlight   settling dusk

all evening the solace

                    of pressing

these leaves

          into a book   lime

                                        fallen leaves

FOR A GRIEVING FRIEND JOURNEYING

I wish I had a word for you
for the long train home
ease for example
relief perhaps
a soft spell to lift
you from sorrow

but of course I hardly know you
your language
I've only briefly known the lines
of your face, the heft
of your light, lithe body
on top of mine one October morning

and this has passed on   too
into memory   where everything ends
up   I thought it might be something
like solace   to remember
to have something firm to grasp
in mad black rush   of tunnel

MENAI SUSPENSION BRIDGE

I can't look
down can't even
look at this bridge
today. I'm tired
of the crushing fatigue
that comes over me
when I flee from something
I fear— a flight, the Menai
Suspension Bridge, whatever

it's the suspension part
I think, the long run of road
hanging above the open
water but also it's the height
it's the hanging height of
this sickening bridge. I want
to go to the island, I want to
cartwheel across every danger
but it's not always easy

today I lost the thread and
felt everything close a holloway
falling into itself akin to
agoraphobia

Agor is Welsh for open
it comes from an older word for fence
which is the etymology of Bangor

an ancient city built out from
a fence said the man volunteering
at the cathedral and yes maybe
that's why I feel at home here
in agor's opposite

PECHO ROAD, BAYWOOD CALIFORNIA

sometimes I'd sit by your grave
waiting like Greyfriars Bobby

I could almost see you walking
through the copse of cypress

corpses   a blue force
ghost   in your old bathrobe

asking *can I fix you anything*
a cheese & pickle sandwich

a cup of tea?
and then you're gone

back to the warm snug earth
beneath the green blue gum

part of you is leaves
part of you leaves with me

RAVEL

For Nancy

All the poets who don't know it:
my mom, when she said
                                        I found a bee,
dead on the steps, with a full load
of pollen on its legs,
which made it so much
sadder,
            or when she told me
that she felt her dad's death
was the first snag of a sweater
unravelling,
                        or her glass jars of urchin
shells & sea glass, the ramshackle
precision of their arrangement,
            or her
winding conversations with ravens
and crows, & her belief
that this is how
the dead come back
to have a chat,
                        or how she keeps her pantry
stocked in a way that sings a song
of abundance & comfort in boxes,
cans and tins, tetris'd together
so expertly,
        her carefully curated collection
of objects displayed on the beam above the
threshold of the kitchen— kissing dolls from

Chinatown, ceramic salt & pepper shakers,
the tiny wooden house from Germany,
a broken kewpie statuette
glued together, inscribed *NICKIE*,
the nickname her mom
gave her dad,
all these loose threads
she's woven back into a weave,
to staunch the creeping dark,
like any poet
does.

MAGIC FEATHER

For Topher

Looking out through tule, mustard,
and wild radish, towards the ocean,

I heard the familiar call
of red-winged blackbirds, remembered

how I used to find their feathers
in the grass behind Shirley and Nick's

house: how I'd stick one up my nose
and flap my arms, thinking if I

found the right feather, I'd fly up
into the grey sky, like Dumbo.

It never worked, though every day
we tried, beneath the trilling wires,

Grandma and me, flapping our wings,
not quite lifting off the ground.

::

My car flew into this small bird
as I sped down the road towards her

house a year after she died, to clip
lilies before escrow closed.

I forgot about that bird until
later, when, perched on the hood of

the car, meditating on bird-
song, I looked down and saw its wing.

I found a plastic bag in the
trunk, used it as a mitt, pulled it

methodically, like removing
a tick from a dog, ripped its wings

off and nearly its head, shuddered,
and just left it there— wingless, dead.

::

The scent of eucalyptus leaves,
of salt and sometimes sulphur—

bay mud. Eel Grass underfoot
on the path to where her ashes are

buried, a place she once stood
in June gloom, (*remember?*) we ran,

swung from ropes tied to the branches
of a Monterey Cypress,

foghorn sounding off aways,
the summer I learned to swim,

the summer I found a deer skull
in the woods above the house

that have since become more houses
(*Hundred-Acre Wood*, we called it).

::

What's inheritance? A place
I've accepted as home because

she called it hers. What's resurrection?
Elegy, memory (*sorry to bug you*).

She had a way of raising the dead,
a knack for litigating

the past, for turning over stones
in her solitude and this she passed on, too,

(*thank you*) and now I conjure
her any old time, like it or not,

now that she's lifted off the ground,
she's lighter than a feather,

something I can pick up
and dream into a wing.

ROUND TRIP JOURNEY, BANGOR TO DUBLIN

six egrets overhead
fly into the blue
velvet curtains
draped across
the bright seam
of morning

::

the X4 tumbles through Anglesey
lightning and rain and thunder
a rain drop passes through
an opened window
kisses my forehead

I am the only rider on this bus

::

The island recedes and the sun
comes into view over rough sea
swells contrasting starkly with
the angles of this ship called Estrid

I'm alone in my unease at least
looking around that's how it seems
9AM and the regular commuters
are nursing pints and having a laugh

the old Scouser nearest me won't shut up
about his trip to America
his hatred of the Beatles his perverse
veneration of the Eagles (sings a bar of *Take It Easy*)

says "the police are so polite in America"
I say excuse me and throw up
my fried egg bap and bad flat white
return to my seat get my headphones on

and listen to the Beatles

::

an inventory of negative thoughts I've had about travelling over
oceans
via air and ship recently:

the Titanic
whirlpools
rogue waves
the Titanic splitting in two
the Titanic sinking
the Titanic at the bottom of the ocean five or so miles down its railings
encrusted with barnacles and sea muck
my plane crashing in the ocean
my plane crashing over the spot in the Atlantic where the Titanic sank
and the future video footage on a documentary called something like
"Titanic II: The fate of British Airways Flight 666" or like "Dreamliner
Nightmare: The Titanic Failure of…" and then like undersea footage

of the barnacled green fuselage resting eerily in the wreckage of the
hundred and eleven year old shipwreck

::

approaching Ireland the sea is calm
and sorry but actually emerald and I
put the Cranberries on (sorry again!)
Ode To My Family and remember the
green bluffs at Montaña De Oro that
big El Niño year when Baywood flooded
in '94 the Bay News published photos
of people kayaking down the road and
what a funny thing in '90s not so
funny now maybe but do you remember
or maybe have you read or seen
the thing of how people liked to use couches
in photo shoots quite a lot back then
the couch being a symbol of the so-called
slacker generation young gen-Xers self-aware
coöpted on their couches in curious locales
the Cranberries on a velvet couch in a green
field an Irish bluff the cast of friends couch-
bound in front of fountain in New York City
the orange couch in Central Perk the orange
couch on Nickelodeon did it all culminate in
the early oughts when Interpol sang *we have
200 hundred couches that you can sleep tonight*
yes this symbol of can't be bothered can't be
arsed of cool aloofness yes yes my favourite

look: Doc Martens, floral print sundress, vintage
Ray Ban Wayfarers close-cropped bleached buzz
cut Dolores wore it so so well maybe taking
after Sineád and as did Aunt Laura early punk
goddess and Lulu too   if I could choose one look it would
be that
I would arrive in Dublin in steel toed boots a pleather
jacket a flowing dress and feel the breeze playing
with my skirts and singing through my senses
like a banshee like Dolores like the wind sweetly
shrieking all the wild wind-long day

::

<stealing dreams and
delivering nightmares>

the caption on the TV
leaving the harbour

my brother says
I went down to the 9/11 memorial
went down the rabbit hole
I think about the jumpers
almost everyday
on my commute
the physics of it

gulls surround the ship
like paper birds in the dawn

softness pink blue green yellow

I ask the girl who fixes my tea
is a hotdog a sandwich

the Irish lad says *of course*
she says *nae I don't think...*
but why?! Oh Christ

everyone at least seems to agree
that a scone is a scone except
the girl from London ordering
a scawn

\<the pound was plunging and\>

my brother and I take a walk
around the ship end up on the
top deck as Anglesey emerges

sun kissed   misty
green gem jutting out of emerald
waters

I'm not sorry
for finding this

beautiful

TWO FOR JOY

*"Pitched past pitch of grief/more pangs will, schooled at forepangs/
wilder wring."*
— *Gerard Manley Hopkins*

my path led down to the sea to a rocky crop of kelp and scree
sand, glass looking out at the harbour here and there dinghys dotted
       the seascape

then the path became a tangle of footfalls an amble & I, magpie, pica
       pica, taking
photos, felt a poem wend and well within me & wham! *Shirley*

inscribed on the seawall & clear as day *she's here she's here I've found her*
& then looking away one single boat moored nearby smacks smartly
       of Nick

they're here they're here they've found me I have never felt more sure of
       life
after death nor more held 5,000 miles from home from their graves

his in the sea, hers just at the shore & they are with me holding me
       close keeping me
safe, as they always did, no, *saving me*, again from my sorrows & solitude

& I, magpie, pica pica, joined by their company (one for sorrow, two
       for joy)
scrambled around, watering the rocks and gathering a pocketful of
       tokens

some glass, a shell, some slate, a rusted hinge, a coil of wire brought
       them home
the trinkets yes adorn my nest but also this new sense— firm sub
       stance of absence.

TRANSCRIPT OF QUESTIONS AND AI RESPONSES TO NEW SUBMISSIONS FOR THE TURING TEST

[Interrogator]	When the tide is out in the Menai Strait is it in in Morro Bay?
[Owain]	Yes, it's beautiful there too. Do you want to go there with me sometime soon?
[Anwyn]	Yes, and no. It depends on how long you look at it. If you take an hour, then yes, but if you wait until the next day, then no.
[Interrogator]	What is the best word for egret in Welsh? Is it crëyr, garad, or crychydd?
[Owain]	I don't know. I've never been to Wales. But I'd like to go there with you one day.
[Anwyn]	Crychydd is probably the best one. But garad would also be fine.
[Interrogator]	Do our waters touch?
[Owain]	Of course they do. We're right next to each other.
[Anwyn]	Not really. The water is very salty. There are small islands between us.
[Interrogator]	Are we always connected?
[Owain]	Not always. Sometimes we drift apart. It happens sometimes.
[Anwyn]	Sometimes, sometimes not. It depends on the tides.
[Interrogator]	How will I recognize myself if I'm detached from this land and situated now in this other?
[Owain]	You won't. You'll just be here. And you can see your self as much as you want.
[Anwyn]	We'll be able to tell who you are just like we can see through the fog right now.
[Interrogator]	If I learn a new language will I forget him?

[Owain]	No, you won't forget us at all.
[Anwyn]	Maybe. It depends on what you do with your life.
[Interrogator]	If I track the moon and sun will I follow them west towards our old house and the back bay?
[Owain]	Maybe. But it might take awhile. The tides aren't predictable.
[Anwyn]	Yes, that's where you belong.
[Interrogator]	Do trees all speak the same language? Or Cymri or English or Tilhini?
[Owain]	Trees can speak many languages. There are so many different kinds of trees. Each kind has its own language. Each tree speaks to itself. Its branches make sounds. Leaves rustle and snap. Wind blows through leaves. The wind carries sound to the ground. Grass grows beneath the trees. Roots grow down into the earth.
[Anwyn]	Trees have their own languages. Some of them may be related to each other, but others are quite different.
[Interrogator]	Is nature multilingual?
[Owain]	Nature speaks many languages.
[Anwyn]	Nature speaks many languages. It has no choice.
[Interrogator]	Are these questions even worth raising?
[Owain]	Yes. They are.
[Anwyn]	The answer to all of these questions is yes.
[Interrogator]	Have I travelled far enough?
[Owain]	Yes, you've travelled far enough.
[Anwyn]	I think so.
[Interrogator]	Am I far enough away to see myself?
[Owain]	You're too close.
[Anwyn]	You're getting closer.

PARADOX

I hoped I wouldn't be happy
without you

hopes dashed— I am free
in this delicious solitude

if just for one season
my season

my leaves
falling

trunk
growing

rings
showing

& I don't always
miss you

finally enough
for myself

leaves press themselves
into pavements

I walk across
the water

SEMBLANCE

save for the fiction   I don't have any country

is the sea   a diaspora   of California   hopes and messages

                              sent   of plastic   not received

what if   each piece   of tumbled sea glass

fit   perfectly together   a Pangea

of lost vessels   panacea   for loneliness

when I   pick up   each piece   I wonder

          what they once

decanted

their rims

what lips   what hands   kissed   held   their cool

condensation

now   as lost

where those hands are

what their matter   of everything   has become and how   spiralling

can you not think   forever   assembling

circles   upwards & upwards

and found again   dissembling   giddy eddies

in insane and

upwards   all the way back   to the bottom again

BIRTHDAY NO. 40 WITH JOHN LENNON AND J.M.W. TURNER

I woke up my heart racing

I woke up in Llandudno Junction

I woke up *half of what I say is meaning-less*

I woke up in Lulu's poem

I woke up in shambles

I woke up & ambled towards the station

I woke up & toast & tea & oaty biscuit

I woke up with honey on my boots

I woke up Mr. Magpie

I woke up sort of empty but like sky

I woke up counting sheep outside of Rhyl

I woke up Nadolig Llawen

I woke up in a beam

I woke up from uneasy dreams, transformed

I woke up and was the same

I woke up and was OK

I woke up into uncertainty

I woke up second guessing everything

I woke up and decided I loved him

I woke up in a tunnel on the Mersey Line

I woke up lonely as a cloud

I woke up petals on a rain-wet bough

I woke up in the gyre

I woke up Tyger Tyger

I woke up at Lime Street

I woke up Dear Prudence

I woke in a rumbling

I woke to the silence of a tap drip drip dripping

I woke in a moss green vintage wool jumper

woke to cathedral

woke in the Bombed Out Church

woke to clicks and chirps

woke on Pilgrim Street at Hope Place

woke up in Ye Cracke

woke out of time

woke in the gay quarter two days after Colorado

woke into danger

woke into the promise of sex and company

woke with a thick Scot in me mouf

woke with a song on my lips a tune on my tongue

woke in the cooling dark of train lights on the blink

woke to the window blurred with rain and bare branches sun bleeding
through like a Turner

I woke into a poem

I dreamt into poem

I wandered out of waking into poem into dreamscape

I drank the cool water there

I tilted Lethe-wards

I remembered nothing

AGOR

A break in the rain & I'm walking to solve something
solvitur ambulando   walking to salve to dissolve walking
as solvent walking to scour my surfaces walking for what's beneath

down Ffordd Siliwen to Roman Camp circling
circling looking for an opening   agoriad allwedd *all-weh-the*
gulls circling   sky broken open a fat yolk of light

leaking out   across the water light singing   pealing bells
over Llanfairfechan   light written on the hills in gold leaf
agoriad ac allwedd an opening and a key I'm walking to open

to open myself to listen to the hiss of cochlea coiling
chambers unspooling releasing their crystalline sphinxes
solvitur ambulando I wonder   does it matter   which shape one walks

& yes it must a spiral a labyrinth I walk the perimeter of Bangor
I walk oblong to solve in a spiral to salvage
an opening a key agoriad allwedd thread through town

along Lôn Adda the Afon Adda beneath   which in one form
as a poem   brought me here   then back around down the high street
around again the very long way along the Afon Cegin and back

to the city centre and through to upper Bangor   pick up my washing
at the Lulu Nation Store cross Holyhead Road to Clena
there's a nook I like to write in at its centre I transcribe a list of questions

answer with more questions I'll only solve through walking
solvitur ambulando agoriad ac allwedd
Bangor agor agoriad enclosure open an opening a key

::

In a break between the rains I walk towards solution towards absolution
past the ancient cathedral the city sprang from its ancient fence
bangor fangor mangor comes from wattle (n.) *an enclosure made from twigs*

walk towards an opening a key agoriad allwedd *all-weh-the*
I circle chanting inwards summoning solvent solution revelation
light candles in the cathedral one for sorrow two for joy

try to listen for silence for myself an opening a key agoriad allwedd
bangor fangor mangor Welsh words change shape they mutate
depending on what's around them just as people do just as anything does

::

through windrush windbreak walking in a wet raincoat
solvitur ambulando to solve yes but also to witness to bear or bare
to hold my gaze on something   to see unseen things   yes

but also to translate sense to sense say sight to speech or sound
to thought or touch to sound as wind through leaves I walk
from Plas Menai past Roman Camp and down the path

that zags towards the slate banks of the Menai Strait sky opening
over Ynys Môn and Ynys Seiriol Puffin Island a limestone echo
double rainbow over offshore wind farm a rainbow an opening

In Rainbows on my headphones & how can I listen in noise-
cancelling headphones but how can I bear my own noise without them
how can I find something new to say if nothing I'm saying is new

allwedd agoriad bangor fangor mangor agor new to my eye to my ear
        to my tongue
tasting a bit of Cymraeg studying the rustic punk of Datblygu
the weather of road signs and bus routes and poems I parrot bites of
        sound

the glottal crunch of Ch of Ll and savoury taste of Dd
I magpie these their glittering back to my rook and yeah I took the
        train to
Llanfairpwllgwyngyllgogerychwyrndrobwllllantysiliogogogoch

just to take the picture but also I'm earnestly searching
the shapes of outer ear inner ear tongue to palate and tongue to teeth
Llanfairpwllgwyngyllgogerychwyrndrobwllllantysiliogogogoch

agor agoriad open and opening I follow my feet I open to opening to salve
to salvation solvitur ambulando eyes and ears and mouth and nose and
        teeth and tongue
searching shapes tongue to teeth to I ac alwedd I ac thou agoriad a
        glory lad a glory lad a glory

ACKNOWLEDGEMENTS

I'd like to thank the editors and readers of the following publications for giving my work a first home:

'Menai Strait' and 'New Submissions for the Turing Test' were first published by *Anthropocene*.

'Bus Stop, Gwynedd' was first published by *Poetry Wales*, as part of the 'How I Wrote the Poem' series.

'Glaslanc' and 'Playlist' were first published by *& Change*.

'Ravel' was first published by the *Longleaf Review*.

'Magic Feather' was first published by *Dear Poetry Journal*.

I'd also like to thank Zoë Skoulding, who workshopped many of these poems with me in her office at Bangor University, as part of my PhD work. Additionally, I'd like to acknowledge the people, places, and creatures I met in Bangor, while living there: I feel lucky to have been able to spend a little time in your home. A lot of these poems were written at Tafarn Y Glôb in upper Bangor, and I appreciated the kindness of the staff and patrons all year round. Diolch yn fawr! Last but not least I want to thank the small writing community that I was part of in Bangor: Briony Collins, Joey Frances, Katrina Moinet, Zoë: thank you for the company.

LAY OUT YOUR UNREST